Spellathon
Book 3

www.pegasusforkids.com

© **B. Jain Publishers (P) Ltd.** All rights reserved. No part of this book may be reproduced, stored in a retrieval system or transmitted, in any form or by any means, mechanical, photocopying, recording or otherwise, without any prior written permission of the publisher.

Published by Kuldeep Jain for B. Jain Publishers (P) Ltd., D-157, Sector 63, Noida - 201307, U.P.
Registered office: 1921/10, Chuna Mandi, Paharganj, New Delhi-110055

Printed in India

CONTENTS

A AND B 4

C AND D 7

E AND F 9

G AND H 11

I AND J 13

K AND L 15

M AND N 18

O AND P 20

Q AND R 22

S AND T 24

U, V AND W 26

X, Y AND Z 29

HOMOPHONES 31

PLURALS 32

APPENDIX: SIGHT WORDS 34

ANSWERS 35

A AND B

1. Match the following:

a. Aircraft
   Aercraft
   Ayrcraft

b. Bren
   Bran
   Brain

c. Aligator
   Alligater
   Alligator

d. Baluns
   Balloons
   Balluns

e. Archer
   Aercher
   Archur

f. Basket
   Bascket
   Backet

g. Avard
   Award
   Awarrd

h. Buffalo
   Bafalo
   Bufallo

i. Ankor
   Ancher
   Anchor

j. Brije
   Brige
   Bridge

Date: _____   Teacher's Signature: _____

2. Arrange the following letters to make meaningful words:

   a. Y G A N R

   (Hint: A person who is not happy.)

   b. I R L P A

   (Hint: The fourth month of the year.)

   c. T O T M B O

   (Hint: Base or lowest level.)

   d. G U U A T S

   (Hint: The eighth month of the year.)

   e. E W E E N B T

   (Hint: In the middle.)

   f. P T A I O R R

   (Hint: Place where planes land and take-off from.)

   g. I B D I L N U G

   (Hint: A place where people live.)

Teacher's Signature: _____ Date: _____

3. Choose the correct words to fill in the blanks:

   a. Mona _____ (axed/asked) her brother for his pencil.

   b. The boy sat down ____ (beside/beeside) the tree.

   c. Dan shut the door with a ____. (bong/bang)

   d. I met Shiela _____ (after/aefter) I left the house.

   e. I like to spread _____ (bitter/butter) on my toast.

Words to Remember

A Aching, Acting, Addition, Aeroplane, After, Album, Alligator, Already, Angry, Another, Anyway, Apartment, Aping, Apply, Archer, Artist, Asked, Autumn, Award, Aware

B Balloon, Bamboo, Bang, Barter, Basket, Before, Belong, Beside, Between, Blame, Bland, Border, Boring, Boss, Bother, Bottom, Bracket, Branch, Bring, Brother, Burglar, Butterfly, Buyer

Date: _____   Teacher's Signature: _____

C AND D

1. Match the Following:

    a. Doctor

    b. Clown

    c. Dish

    d. Dragon

    e. Cloud

    f. Cricket

    g. Drink

    h. Computer

    i. Cat

    j. Dove

Teacher's Signature: _____

Date: _____

2. Look at the pictures and tick the correct spellings:

a. Claw

   Clo

   Clau

b. Dram

   Drum

   Drem

c. Dentist

   Dontest

   Dintist

d. Klok

   Cloak

   Cloake

e. Chyn

   Chin

   Cin

f. Duve

   Dove

   Dave

3. Make new words using the letters in the hexagon. Try to make a word using all the letters:

   _____   _____

   _____   _____

   _____   _____

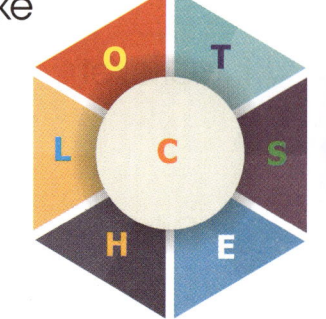

Words to Remember

C Cage, Camping, Cast, Certain, Chain, Chamber, Change, Chapter, Chatter, Child, Clang, Clap, Class, Claw, Climb, Clinic, Cloud, Clutter, Coach, Cocoa, Complain, Computer, Country, Cover, Crafts, Crate,

D Does, Dove, Deck, Dock, Drove, Drink, Danger, Dark, Damp, Dart, Daily, Doubt, Dream, Dummy, During, Drown, Dodge, Dagger, Dubbed, Dull, Dupe

Date: _____   Teacher's Signature: _____

E AND F

1. Match the boxes in column A with those in column B to form words. One has been done as an example:

A	B
a. eng	ugh
b. fol	ning
c. ex	ily
d. eve	lent
e. fln	low
f. feb	lish
g. excel	ruary
h. eno	ish
i. fam	cept

Teacher's Signature: _____   Date: _____

2. These pictures start with the letter E or F. Name them and put them in the right column:

A	B

3. Synonyms are the words that mean the same. Tick the synonyms of the following words:

   a. Well known: Farmer   Famous   Fashion
   b. Come inside: Eager   Easter   Enter
   c. Very happy: Elated   Ethnic   Ending
   d. Weak: Fairy   Erupt   Frail
   e. Complete: Finish   Enter   Engage

Words to Remember

 Each, Eager, Eagle, Early, Easter, Easy, Ebony, Echo, Eel, Eighteen, Eighty, Elated, Elephant, Emotion, Enact, Ending, Engage, English, Enough, Enter, Erupt, Escape, Ethnic, Every, Everywhere, Excellent, Excited, Exercise

 Factory, Fair, Fairy, Famous, Fancy, Fare, Farming, Father, Favour, Fever, Fewer, Fifteen, Fifty, Fight, Finance, Fingers, Finish, First, Fishing, Fist, Foil, Follow, Force, Forever, Forge, Forget, Frail, Frame, Frank, Freckles, Fresh

Date: _____   Teacher's Signature: _____

G AND H

1. What's in the box? Choose from the words given below:

> Handcuffs   Hockey   Grasshopper   Giant   Guitar
> Hippopotamus   Gorilla   Grenade   Girl   Hanger   Ground
> Host   Growl   Height   Horse

_____

_____

_____

_____

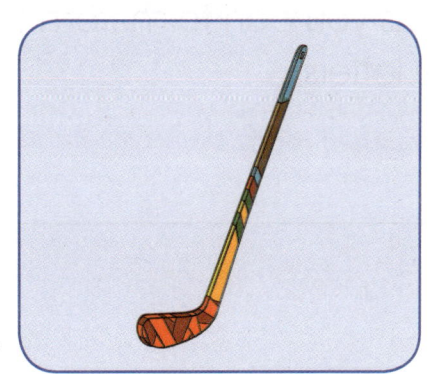
_____

_____

_____

Teacher's Signature: _____   Date: _____

2. Find the missing letters:
   a. G A T H __ R
   b. H O N __ U R
   c. H __ S B __ N D
   d. G R __ U N D
   e. H O __ E Y

3. Circle the wrong spellings in the following sentences, and write the correct spellings:

   a. I like to eat green gripes.

   b. There are many guaves on the tree.

   c. I am feeling very hongry.

   d. My bag was very hevey.

   e. We should plant seeds in the gruond.

   f. My brother was very hapie to see me.

4. Let's see how many words you can form from the following words. Each word must have at least three letters.

   a. GRANDMOTHER
   _____

   b. HOMEWORK
   _____

Words to Remember

G Gape, Gash, Gather, Give, Gleam, Glow, Gnaw, Goal, Goddess, Gown, Grab, Ground, Group, Grove, Guard, Guava, Guide, Guitar

H Half, Happy, Harmless, Have, Health, Heat, Heavy, Hedge, Hence, Hidden, Higher, Hippopotamus, Home, Honey, Hope, Horn, Horrible, Horse, House, Hundred, Hungry, Hurry

Date: _____   Teacher's Signature: _____

I AND J

1. Find the following in the Word Grid:

Jellyfish	Joker	Jersey	Island
Insect	Igloo	Juice	

A	D	J	U	I	C	E	F	T
W	H	R	I	G	L	O	O	Q
S	J	V	S	W	I	V	G	F
J	E	L	L	Y	F	I	S	H
O	R	Y	A	M	X	R	N	Y
K	S	I	N	S	E	C	T	V
E	E	C	D	P	Q	B	W	X
R	Y	E	L	K	A	X	H	J

2. Fill in the blanks by solving the jumbled words. You may take help from words given below:

| INSIDE | INSTEAD | JUDGE | IMPORTANT |
| IGNORE | JUICE | JANUARY | INDIA |

a. My mother gave me a milkshake _____ (SEATDNI) of plain milk.

b. The cat is _____ (EISDNI) the box.

c. The _____ (EJGUD) punishes thieves.

d. The first month of the year is _____ (RNYAJUA).

e. Delhi is the capital of _____ (NIIAD).

f. I love drinking apple _____ (ECJIU).

g. I never _____ (GINROE) what my teachers say.

h. It is _____ (AMTPNROIT) to tell the truth.

Words to Remember

I — Idea, Ideal, Igloo, Ignore, Illegal, Immune, Important, Indian, Injure, Insert, Inside, Instead, Interest, Island

J — Jail, January, Jeans, Jersey, Jewel, Joke, Judge, Juice, July, Jumped, June, Jute

Date: _____ Teacher's Signature: _____

K AND L

1. Fill in the blanks:

a. _ N _ F _

b. L _ _ P

c. K _ _ B _ AR _

d. L _ _ A _ D

e. _ N E _

f. _ O _ K

g. K _ NG _ R _ _

h. _ E _ _ A _ D

i. K _ _ E

j. _ O _ _ S

Teacher's Signature: _____   Date: _____

k. K _ _ T _ _

l. _ E _ O _

m. _ I _ T _ _

n. L _ _ S _ _ R

2. Use the first letters of the names of every picture to make new words:

a.     =

___ ___ ___ ___   ___

b.      =

___ ___ ___ ___ ___ ___   ___

c.       =

___ ___ ___ ___ ___ ___   ___

d.      =

___ ___ ___ ___ ___ ___   ___

Date: _____   Teacher's Signature: _____

e.      = ____
___ ___ ___ ___ ___ ___

f.       = ____
___ ___ ___ ___ ___ ___

g.   11   = ____
___ ___ ___ ___ ___

3. Fill in the blanks with the right word:

  a. We cook food in the _____. (kitcen/kitchen)

  b. Hina has very _____ (lung/long) hair.

  c. Jia is the wicket _____ (keeper/keepare) of our cricket team.

  d. Our midday meal is known as _____. (launch/lunch)

  e. Jokes make me _____. (laugh/leugh)

Words to Remember

K Kangaroo, Karate, Keen, Keeper, Kick, King, Kit, Kitchen, Kite, Kiwi, Knee, Kneel, Knew, Knife, Knight, Knit

L Ladder, Laugh, Lawyer, Lazy, Leaf, Leap, Leather, Leave, Leopard, Letter, Lever, Liar, Lion, Listen, Lively, Lizard, Long, Love, Lovely, Lower, Lumber, Lunch,

Teacher's Signature: _____   Date: _____

M AND N

1. Compound words are formed when two different words are joined together. Underline the words in the second column to make compound words. Remember, you can have more than one compound word in each row:

Mail	Box	Man	Ring
News	Pipe	Paper	Kind
Net	House	Case	Work
Match	Row	Box	Long
Man	Kind	Hole	Made
Note	Pad	Book	Line
Mad	Hand	Paper	House

2. Guess the missing letter:

   a. M _ R C H

   b. M E _ S A G E

   c. N I _ E T E E N

   d. N E _ S P A P E R

   e. N A _ I O N

   f. M E _ B E R

   g. _ I S T A K E

   h. N O T H I _ G

   i. M Y S _ L F

   j. N O V E _ B E R

   k. N E C E S S _ R Y

   l. M I N _ T E

   m. M O R N I _ G

   n. M Y S T _ R Y

   o. N E I _ H E R

   p. N E R _ O U S

Date: _____   Teacher's Signature: _____

3. Antonyms are the words that are opposite in meaning. For example, Happy is the opposite of Sad. Thus, they are antonyms. Select the words that mean the opposite of the following:

a. Tiny:	Mini	Massive	Nervous
b. Silence:	Maple	Noose	Noise
c. Everything:	Nothing	Mimic	Nobody
d. Side:	Moss	Middle	Navy
e. Day:	Manger	Numb	Night

Words to Remember

 Magic, Mammoth, Manager, Manger, Mango, Maple, March, Market, Massive, Measure, Member, Message, Middle, Milk, Mimic, Minute, Mistake, Money, Monster, More, Morsel, Moss, Mouse, Movie, Music

Nail, Name, Nature, Navy, Nervous, Night, Nineteen, Ninety, Nobody, Noise, Noose, North, Nose, Nothing, Nugget, Numb, Number, Nuzzle

Teacher's Signature: _____   Date: _____

O AND P

1. These zoo animals, birds and sea creatures have escaped! Help the zoo keeper find them. Write down the names of the birds in the tree, animals in the cage and the sea animals in the little pond:

Ostrich	Peacock	Owl	Octopus	Orca
Penguin	Parrot	Pigeon	Porcupine	Python

2. Join the two to form a new word:

   a. 🫛 + Cock = _____

   b. Oar + 🔒 = _____

   c. Oil + 📚 = _____

   d. Pop + 🌽 = _____

Date: _____   Teacher's Signature: _____

e. Out + 🚪 = _____

f. 🖊 + guin = _____

g. 🐷 + eon = _____

h. Police + 👨 = _____

3. Replace the underlined letters with either O or P to form new words:

   a. S P I K E   S P __ K E
   b. B A R R O W   B __ R R O W
   c. J A C K E T   __ __ C K E T
   d. C R E A K   C R __ A K
   e. G R A T E   G R A __ E
   f. S T R I K E   S T R I __ E
   g. C L A V E R   C L __ V E R
   h. S C A N N E R   S __ A N N E R

Words to Remember

O — Oak, Oats, Object, Ocean, October, Office, Officer, Often, Okra, Older, Orange, Order, Ostrich, Other, Otter, Outside, Over, Owner

P — Packing, Pale, Pants, Parrot, Partner, Party, Patch, Pearl, Penguin, Pest, Pickle, Pinch, Plans, Plenty, Pocket, Pole, Porridge, Power, Practice, Pretty, Princess, Problem, Punch, Purpose

Teacher's Signature: _____   Date: _____

Q AND R

1. Unjumble the following words:

a. ENEUQ _____	b. SORTORE _____
c. TQLIU _____	d. BROBIN _____
e. USEIQTNO _____	f. RTEEACGNL _____
g. UVIQRE _____	h. ONOACRC _____
i. RQATUER _____	j. CTOREK _____

QUARTER ROCKET QUIVER RECTANGLE RACCOON
QUEEN RIBBON QUESTION QUILT ROOSTER

Date: _____ Teacher's Signature: _____

2. Find the following words in the word grid:

Across

2. We wear this to protect ourselves from the rain
3. A bird that looks like a crow
6. A baby's toy that makes a noise when shaken
7. Do something very fast
8. A search for something

Down

1. An arch of seven colours that appears after it rains
4. To fight
5. To come back
7. Shaking of the earth

Words to Remember

Q Quadrant, Quake, Quaker, Qualify, Quantify, Quarrel, Quarter, Quest, Question, Queue, Quick, Quicksand, Quiet, Quite

R Raincoat, Rapid, Real, Rectangle, Regal, Regular, Reins, Remark, Remember, Remind, Repair, Report, Respect, Reward, Right

Teacher's Signature: _____   Date: _____

S AND T

1. Match the yellow boxes with the appropriate white boxes to form new words:

SIDE

SPOON   KICK

AFTER

SOME   GIRL

CASTLE   YARD

TAIL

ROOM   ONE

WALL

SAND

ABOUT   CLOTH

WALK

TABLE

SPIN   LIGHT

THING

THERE   PAPER   WHERE

Sidekick   Tailspin   Sandpaper   Tablespoon   Sidewalk
Thereabout   Someone   Sandcastle   Somewhere   Taillight
Sidewall   Something   Tablecloth   Thereafter

Date: _____   Teacher's Signature: _____

2. What happens when you pair S and T with H? We get a brand new sound with Sh and Th. Now find where you can fit these sounds in the following words:

a. ☐ A D O W

b. ☐ A T

c. B I R ☐

d. ☐ U M B

e. ☐ O U L D E R

f. F L U ☐

g. ☐ A R E

h. O ☐ E R

Words to Remember

S — Sack, Said, Salt, Same, Saw, Scare, Scene, Score, Sea, Seat, See, Sell, Send, Sew, Ships, Single, Six, Soap, Sort, Soup, South, Spell, Stair, Stare, Stars, Still, Stool, Stop, Sugar, Summer, Sunday, Swans, Swim

T — Table, Tall, Tame, Tape, Tasty, Teach, Tell, Test, That, Thing, This, Those, Three, Tick-Tock, Tiffin, Tiger, Tile, Till, Tilt, Time, Tin, Tip, Tire, Toffee, Top, Toy, Train, Trap, Trees, Two

Teacher's Signature: _____   Date: _____

U, V AND W

1. What's in the box?

 _____

 _____

 _____

 _____

 _____

Date: _____   Teacher's Signature: _____

_____

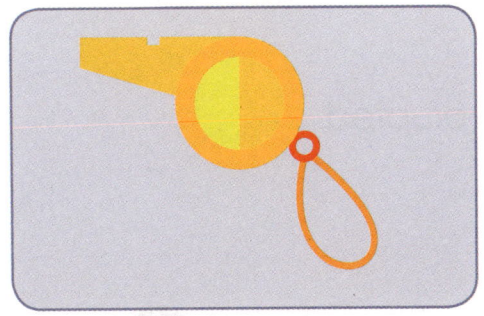

_____

_____

| Vegetables | Whistle | Umbrella | Utensils |
| Unicorn | Vulture | Window | Violin |

2. The following words are missing certain letters. It could be U, V or W. Fill in the missing letters:

a. __ A R I E T Y   b. __ S __ A L

c. C R E __   d. G R O __ N D

e. D R A __   f. B R A __ E

g. A __ N T Y   h. B L O __

i. B L __ N T   j. __ E I G H T

k. __ I S I T   l. A C T I __ E

m. A D __ I S E   n. M O __ T H

o. __ I E R D

Teacher's Signature: _____   Date: _____

3. The following sentences have some words that are spelled wrongly. Correct the wrong words:

   a. She has a very loud vocie.

   b. Cats have very long whiskres.

   c. My mother's brother is my ucnle.

   d. It is easier to walk downhill than uphile.

   e. There was an earthquake before the vulcano erupted.

Words to Remember

U Umbrella, Uncertain, Uncle, Understand, Unhappy, Unicorn, Uniform, Unreal, Uphill, Uptown, Usual

V Vague, Vain, Value, Vase, Vegetable, Veins, Vest, Video, View, Violin, Visit, Vivid, Voice, Volcano, Vote, Vow

W Wand, Warn, Watch, Wave, Weather, Weave, Whale, Wheat, Whether, Which, While, Whisk, Whisker, Whistle, Wipe, Wisdom, Wise, Wonder, Worry, Wrong

Date: _____   Teacher's Signature: _____

X, Y AND Z

1. Find the following:
   - 4 words starting with X
   - 3 words starting with Y
   - 4 words starting with Z

Y	A	R	D	S	T	I	C	K
O	X	O	P	Z	E	B	R	A
L	R	X	W	I	F	F	W	X
K	A	Y	T	P	C	L	Q	Z
X	Y	L	O	P	H	O	N	E
M	B	E	Y	E	A	R	Z	R
A	P	M	D	R	V	J	X	O
S	Z	U	C	C	H	I	N	I

X: _____

Y: _____

Z: _____

X-Mas	Yolk	Zebra	Xylophone
Yardstick	X-Ray	Zipper	Year
Zucchini	Xylem	Zero	

Teacher's Signature: _____   Date: _____

2. Listen to the story and fill in the blanks with the right words:

Jia and Tony loved all the seasons of the _____ (your/year). They loved _____ (winter/wintre) because they had holidays for _____ (X-Mas/X-Ray). This year, their family decided to visit the _____ (zoo/zeu) on Christmas. Jia liked watching the lions, but Tony thought the _____ (zebras/zebars) were the best. On their way home, the _____ (whole/while) family ate _____ (yummy/youmy) sandwiches. Jia's _____ (younger/yonger) sister is just a baby. She slept through the whole trip!

3. Make new words from the following:

a. Xylophone

_____

b. Yesterday

_____

c. Zestful

_____

Words to Remember

X X-Mas, X-Ray, Xylem X-axis, Xylophone

Y Yacht, Year, Yearend, Yearn, Yeast, Yellow, Yelp, Yesterday, Yolk, Young, Youth, Youthful

Z Zany, Zeal, Zebra, Zesty, Zigzag, Zinnia, Zipper, Zone, Zoo, Zucchini

Date: _____   Teacher's Signature: _____

HOMOPHONES

Sometimes two words can sound similar and yet have different meanings. They are called homophones. Pick the right word in each sentence:

1. There is a _____ in the garden. (bee/be)

2. We have one _____ to finish the homework. (hour/our)

3. I want to _____ what the teacher is saying. (hear/here)

4. Father went to _____ vegetables. (by/buy)

5. Sara's letter came in the _____ today. (mail/male)

6. My _____ looks like my father's. (knows/nose)

7. Neel went to _____ his friend. (meet/meat)

8. The _____ is really bright today. (son/sun)

9. This is a _____ plate. (steal/steel)

10. Meera lives in a two _____ building. (storey/story)

11. We can make _____ mistakes in an exam. (know/no)

12. Lara and Tom used _____ paper to make their project. (plane/plain)

13. _____ is Seema's copy? (Wear/Where)

14. This chair is made of _____. (wood/would)

15. The horse has a bushy _____. (tale/tail)

16. Ahana _____ the race. (won/one)

Teacher's Signature: _____   Date: _____

PLURALS

We can get most plural forms by simply adding an s at the end of the word. But there are some rules you have to keep in mind:

— Words that end in ch, x, s, z or s-like sounds, add es in their plural forms.

— Words that end in a vowel, followed by a y, add an s in their plural forms.

— Words that end in a consonant, followed by a y, add ies in their plural forms.

— Some words that end in 'o' get an 'es' in their plural forms.

— Words that end in f or fe, add ies in their plural forms.

1. Write the plural forms of the following words:

   a. Snake   _____

   b. Kiss   _____

   c. Watch   _____

   d. Match   _____

   e. Box   _____

   f. Family   _____

   g. Ferry   _____

   h. Mango   _____

   i. Leaf   _____

   j. Loaf   _____

   k. Dear   _____

   l. Bus   _____

   m. Chimney: _____

Date: _____   Teacher's Signature: _____

2. Write the correct spellings:

   a. Foxs _____

   b. Buffalos _____

   c. Heros _____

   d. Lorrys _____

   e. Autoes _____

   f. Potatos _____

   g. Knifes _____

   h. Boyes _____

   i. Snakies _____

   j. Batchs _____

   k. Windoes _____

   l. Archs _____

APPENDIX: SIGHT WORDS

Here are some words that we use very often. Learn a new word every day!

about	funny	them	share	help	side
know	great	were	knife	late	things
shake	house	after	rain	seen	very
joke	going	jump	right	fight	year
before	every	keep	over	sight	help
because	write	might	many	wire	place
another	yours	learn	than	most	work
day	round	much	thank	give	corn
would	think	people	their	cool	through
when	walk	should	want	only	same

Date: _____ Teacher's Signature: _____

ANSWER KEY

A and B

1. a. Aircraft   b. Brain   c. Alligator   d. Balloons   e. Archer
   f. Basket   g. Award   h. Buffalo   i. Anchor   j. Bridge

2. a. Angry   b. April   c. Bottom   d. August   e. Between
   f. Airport   g. Building

3. a. asked   b. beside   c. bang   d. after   e. butter

C AND D

1. a. Doctor
   b. Clown
   c. Dish
   d. Dragon
   e. Cloud
   f. Cricket
   g. Drink
   h. Computer
   i. Cat
   j. Dove

2. a. Claw   b. Drum   c. Dentist   d. Cloak   e. Dove

3. Clot, Those, Shot, Shoe, Chose, Close, Hotel, Clothes

Teacher's Signature: _____   Date: _____

E AND F

1. a. English   b. Follow   c. Except   d. Evening   e. Finish
    f. February   g. Excellent   h. Enough   i. Family

2.
E	F
Elephant	Football
Eighty	Finger
Eagle	Forty
Eye	Frog
Earth	Fork

3. a. Famous   b. Enter   c. Elated   d. Frail   e. Finish

G AND H

1. Girl, Handcuffs, Gorilla, Hippopotamus, Hockey stick, Grasshopper, Guitar

2. a. GATHER   b. HONOUR   c. HUSBAND   d. GROUND   e. HONEY
   f. GUESS

3. a. Grapes   b. Guavas   c. Hungry   d. Heavy   e. Ground
   f. Happy

4. a. Grand, Mother, More, Got, And, The, Den, Dent, Dog, Other, Her, Rang, Rear, etc.

   b. Home, Work, Rook, Hook, Wok, More, Whom, Rome, Room, Worm, Woe, Roe, etc.

Date: _____   Teacher's Signature: _____

I AND J

1.
A	D	J	U	I	C	E	F	T
W	H	R	I	G	L	O	O	Q
S	J	V	S	W	I	V	G	F
J	E	L	L	Y	F	I	S	H
O	R	Y	A	M	X	R	N	Y
K	S	I	N	S	E	C	T	V
E	E	C	D	P	Q	B	W	X
R	Y	E	L	K	A	X	H	J

2. a. Instead   b. Inside   c. Judge   d. January   e. India

   f. Juice   g. Ignore   h. Important

K AND L

1. a. KNIFE   b. LAMP   c. KEYBOARD   d. LIZARD   e. KNEE

   f. LOCK   g. KANGAROO   h. LEOPARD   i. KITE   j. LOTUS

   k. KETTLE   l. LEMON   m. KITTEN   n. LOBSTER

2. a. Know   b. Karate   c. Lizard   d. Lovely   e. Letter

   f. Ladder   g. Keeper

3. a. kitchen   b. long   c. keeper   d. lunch   e. laugh

M AND N

1. a. Mailman, Mailbox   b. Newspaper

   c. Network   d. Matchbox

   e. Mankind, Manhole, Man-made   f. Notepad, Notebook

   g. Madhouse

Teacher's Signature: _____   Date: _____

2. a. MARCH   b. MESSAGE   c. NINETEEN   d. NEWSPAPER   e. NATION
    f. MEMBER g. MISTAKE   h. NOTHING   i. MYSELF   j. NOVEMBER
    k. NECESSARY l. MINUTE m. MORNING   n. MYSTERY   o. NEITHER
    p. NERVOUS

3. a. Massive b. Noise c. Nothing d. Middle e. Night

O AND P

1. Birds: Ostrich, Parrot, Pigeon, Peacock, Owl
    Animals: Porcupine, Python,
    Sea Animals: Octopus, Orca, Penguin

2. a. Peacock b. Oarlock c. Oilcloth, d. Popcorn e. Outdoor
    f. Penguin g. Polestar h. Policeman

3. a. SPOKE b. BORROW c. POCKET d. CROAK e. GRAPE
    f. STRIPE g. CLOVER h. SPANNER

Q AND R

1. a. QUEEN b. ROOSTER c. QUILT d. RIBBON e. QUESTION
    f. RECTANGLE g. QUIVER h. RACCOON i. QUARTER j. ROCKET

2. Crossword:
    - 2 across: RAINCOAT
    - 2 down: RAINBOW
    - 4 across: RAVEN
    - 4 down: QUURAK (Q-U-A-K... reading: Q, U, A, K from down clue 7Q: QUAK...)
    - 6 across: RATTLE
    - 5 down: RETURN
    - 7 across: QUICKLY
    - 8 across: QUEST

S AND T

1. Sidekick, Sidewall, Sidewalk, Something, Someone, Somewhere, Sandcastle, Sandpaper, Taillight, Tailspin, Tablespoon, Tablecloth, Thereabout, Thereafter

2. a. Shadow   b. That   c. Birth   d. Thumb   e. Shoulder
   f. Flush   g. Share   h. Other   i. Thirty   j. Shape

U, V AND W

1. Umbrella, Violin, Vulture, Window, Unicorn, Utensils, Whistle, Vegetables

2. a. VARIETY   b. USUAL   c. CREW   d. GROUND   e. DRAW
   f. BRAVE   g. AUNTY   h. BLOW   i. BLUNT   j. WEIGHT
   k. VISIT   l. ACTIVE   m. ADVISE   n. MOUTH   o. WEIRD

3. a. voice   b. whiskers,   c. uncle,   d. uphill,   e. volcano

X, Y AND Z

1. X: X-Mas, X-Ray, Xylem, Xylophone; Y: Yardstick, Yolk, Year; Z: Zebra, Zipper, Zucchini, Zero

2. Jia and Tony loved all the seasons of the <u>year</u>. They loved <u>winter</u> because they had holidays for <u>X-Mas</u>. This year, their family decided to visit the <u>zoo</u> on Christmas. Jia liked watching the lions, but Tony thought the <u>zebras</u> were the best. On their way home, the <u>whole</u> family ate <u>yummy</u> sandwiches. Jia's <u>younger</u> sister is just a baby. She slept through the whole trip!

HOMOPHONES

1. bee   2. hour   3. hear   4. buy   5. mail
6. nose   7. meet   8. sun   9. steel   10. storey
11. no   12. plain   13. Where   14. wood   15. tail   16. won

Teacher's Signature: _____   Date: _____

PLURALS

1. a. Snakes   b. Kisses   c. Watches   d. Matches   e. Boxes
   f. Families   g. Ferries   h. Mangoes   i. Leaves   j. Loaves
   k. Dears   l. Buses   m. Chimneys

2. a. Foxes   b. Buffaloes   c. Heroes   d. Lorries   e. Autos
   f. Potatoes   g. Knives   h. Boys   i. Snakes   j. Batches
   k. Windows   l. Arches

Date: _____   Teacher's Signature: _____